永嘉画册

从SONG到SONG

中共永嘉县委宣传部 主编

线装书局

图书在版编目（CIP）数据

永嘉画册：从SONG到SONG / 中共永嘉县委宣传部主编. -- 北京：线装书局, 2023.9

ISBN 978-7-5120-5708-1

I. ①永… II. ①中… III. ①永嘉县 - 概况 - 画册

IV. ①K925.54-64

中国国家版本馆CIP数据核字(2023)第168329号

永嘉画册：从SONG到SONG

YONGJIAHUACE:CONGSONGDAOSONG

作　　者：中共永嘉县委宣传部

责任编辑：林菲

出版发行：**线 装 书 局**

地　　址：北京市丰台区方庄日月天地大厦B座17层（100078）

电　　话：010-58077126（发行部）010-58076938（总编室）

网　　址：www.zgxzsj.com

经　　销：新华书店

印　　制：廊坊市新景彩印制版有限公司

开　　本：889mm×1194mm 1/16

印　　张：9.5

字　　数：30千字

版　　次：2023年9月第1版第1次印刷

线装书局官方微信

定　　价：180.00元

YONGJIA CHINA

SONG，听不完的宋韵

永嘉，水长而美，永受嘉福。1800多年的建县史，承载着温州的历史之根、文化之源；

2677.64平方公里，八山一水一分田，山水如画，沁润人文。

S山水成诗、O瓯越传承、N南戏昆韵、G古村古韵，这是永嘉的千年之旅，这是宋韵的不息文脉。

山水成诗
Landscapes Forming Poetry

05. 水长而美 A Long And Beautiful River
13. 山林通幽 Secluded Mountains And Forests
25. 桃源深处 Deep Within The Peach Blossom Land

瓯越传承
Legacy of Ou-Yue

37. 淬火瓯窑 Ouyao Kiln Tempered by Fire
45. 沁心茶食 Refreshing Tea And Cuisine
51. 非遗承袭 Intangible Cultural Heritage

南戏昆韵
61. Southern Drama

古村古韵
Ancient Villages With Ancient Rhymes

73. 耕读传家 Cultivating and Learning for Generations
83. 江南宋村 Jiangnan Song Village

千年一瞬

以文脉之名，诚邀山水朝圣之人

NANXI RIVER

The Nanxi River is located in Yongjia County, northern Wenzhou City, Zhejiang Province, 26 kilometers south of Wenzhou city center. Adjacent to Yandang Mountain to the east and Jinyun Xiandu to the west.

Nanxi River is a national AAAA level tourist area. National level scenic spot, world geological park.

The scenic area is famous for its beautiful water, unique rocks, numerous waterfalls. ancient villages. Known as the eterna landscape poetry and the most beautiful peach blossom land. There are natural scenic resources represented by volcanic rock land forms and the Nanxi River system. There are also cultural landscape resources represented by ancient villages and dwellings, rich type combinations and complete scale aggregation.

A Millennium in a Bli

诗蕴山水
脉脉千年
SONG
是宋韵的回响

千年古县 永嘉

永嘉县，隶属中国浙江省温州市，有着1800多年建县史，是温州的历史之根、文化之源。总面积2677.64平方公里，下辖7街道1镇14乡。

拥有「中国长寿之乡」「中国教玩具之都」「中国泵阀之乡」「中国纽扣之都」「中国拉链之乡」等众多金名片，是浙江省县域面积第四大县，温州市第一大县，也是全国首批沿海对外开放县、中国文化旅游大县、中国千年古县，浙江老革命根据地。

楠溪江位于永嘉县境内，是国家AAAA景区名胜区，世界地质公园，国家级风景区以「水秀、岩奇、瀑多、村古、滩林美」闻名，被誉为「永远的山水诗，醉美的桃花源」，内有以火山岩地貌、楠溪江水系为代表自然风景资源，也以古村落、古民居为代表的人文景观资源，类型组合丰富，规模集聚完整。

山水成诗
Landscapes Form

公元422年至423年，诗人谢灵运任永嘉郡守，遍游永嘉山水，写下了大量山水诗，这些清新自然的山水诗，融真情美景深意于一体，开一代风气之先。楠溪江的山水洗去了谢灵运的满腹愤懑和一身疲惫，奠定了他"山水诗鼻祖"的地位；谢灵运也成就了永嘉"中国山水诗的摇篮"的美名。

谢灵运的歌吟已融入中华传统文化及民族审美意识，1600年来，与楠溪江的山水一起，绽放着绚丽的光芒。王羲之、颜延之、陶弘景、李白、杜甫、孟浩然、苏轼、陆游、袁枚等历代名人也曾在此为官或修行、游历，留下许多名篇佳作和文化遗迹。

楠溪江的山水之美，在于其水秀、岩奇、瀑多、滩林美，更在于人与自然、自然与文化、文化与生活的丝丝交融，这是用时光和天地写就的，最美的诗篇。

From 422 to 423 AD, the poet Xie Lingyun (385-433) served as the magistrate of Yongjia County, where he embarked on extensive journeys through the local landscapes, penning a wealth of poetry inspired by the natural beauty. These fresh and natural poems, blending true emotions, beautiful scenery, and profound meaning, became a pioneering trend of their times. The landscapes of the Nanxi River cleansed Xie of his anger and exhaustion, establishing his position as the "ancestor of landscape poetry". Moreover, Xie's contributions earned Yongjia the esteemed reputation as "the cradle of Chinese landscape poetry."

Xie Lingyun's poems has been integrated into the traditional Chinese culture and national aesthetic consciousness, and has been blooming with brilliant light along with the landscape of Nanxi River for 1600 years. Wang Xizhi, Yan Yanzhi, Tao Hongjing, Li Bai, Du Fu, Meng Haoran, Su Shi, Lu You, Yuan Mei and other famous people in the past also served as officials or practiced and traveled here, leaving many famous poems and cultural relics.

The beauty of Nanxi River lies in its beautiful water, beautiful rocks, numerous waterfalls and beautiful beaches, and more importantly, in the integration of man and nature, nature and culture, culture and life. This is the most beautiful poem written with time and heaven and earth.

图片：楠溪江上

The Nanxi River originates from the southern foot of Kuocang Mountain in the northwest of Yongjia County. The upper reaches are divided into the Da Nanxi and Xiao Nanxi, which converge at Jiuzhang before flowing into the Oujiang River at Sanjiang. The main stream stretches 139.8 kilometers, covering a drainage area of 2,429 square kilometers.

The beauty of the Nanxi River lies in its water – pure, gentle, and invigorating to the senses. Upon examination, the river's sand content is only one ten-thousandth of a gram per cubic meter, meeting the national first-class water standard. It has been acclaimed by experts as "the world's finest water."

The Nanxi River showcases a wealth of ever-changing beauty. Its waters flow gently, creating a rhythmic and lively ambiance. The riverbanks are adorned with picturesque sandy forests, offering a constantly shifting landscape. The upper reaches have rapid water flow, with many canyons and waterfalls; the middle reaches gradually widen, with shallow beaches and deep pools distributed with attractive disorder; the lower reaches are mainly wide alluvial plains, providing the agricultural foundation for many villages in the Nanxi River Basin, with a strong pastoral atmosphere.

This is the mother river of Yongjia, a living legend of flowing water. For thousands of years, it has silently nourished the Chinese people's deep longing for a better life and their sense of belonging. This is Yongjia, where the river is long and beautiful.

借问同舟客，何时到永嘉？

唐·孟浩然

山川之美，古来共谈

「山川之美，古来共谈。高峰入云，清流见底。两岸石壁，五色交辉。青林翠竹，四时俱备。晓雾将歇，猿鸟乱鸣。夕日欲颓，沉鳞竞跃。实是欲界之仙都。」

陶弘景《答谢中书书》

楠溪江流域群山连绵，层峦叠嶂，楠溪江的数十条支流是与一座座山峰共生的。楠溪江西岸有三支主要山脉，山峰约50多座山峰；东岸有七支大小山脉，山峰约40座。

千万年前频繁剧烈的火山岩浆活动造就了这里层层叠叠的岩石风貌，斗转星移，日月轮梭，在大自然鬼斧神工之下，形成了现如今楠溪江山两岸壁立地拔如削林愈的山壁，其造型特征楠溪江两峰壁嵯峨，高耸险峻，洞奇山壁，峰嵘嶙峋，与柔美的楠溪江水景形成强烈对比，奇岩险峰，峡谷深幽，险峰峭壁，飞瀑深潭，构成了层次丰富、动静有致的独特景观。

The beauty of mountains and rivers Shared throughout history

"The beauty of mountains and rivers has always been discussed. Peak into the cloud, clear flow to the bottom. On both sides of the stone wall, the five colors cross. The green forest and the green bamboo are all ready. Dawn fog will rest, ape birds singing. The days are fading and the scales are competing. Reality is the heavenly capital of desire."

——Tao Hongjing, "Reply to Xie Zhongshu's letter"

The Nanxi River basin is surrounded by mountains, and its dozens of tributaries are symbiotic with the peaks. There are three main mountain ranges on the west bank of Nanxi River, with more than 50 peaks. There are seven mountain ranges on the east coast, with about 40 peaks.

Tens of thousands of years ago, frequent and intense volcanic magmatic activities created the layered rock style here, the sun and the moon, under the uncanny work of nature, the formation of today's Nanxi River on both sides of the cliffs the landscape of extraordinary peaks, its modeling features are the mountain walls, high cliffs such as cutting, cave hanging, mountain walls, rugged towering, and the soft Nanxi River water scene forms a strong contrast.

At the same time, Nanxi River precipitous cliffs, deep canyons, cliff peaks, waterfalls and deep pos, constitute a rich level, dynamic and unique landscape.

山中何所有，岭上多白云。

南朝 齐 陶弘景

自言官长如灵运，能使山水似永嘉 ——宋·苏轼

时时处处诗情画意

「读诵之暇，唯以弹琴栽花为乐，遇风日晴和，则汲泉煮茗，挈席开樽，与三知己，啸傲于烟霞泉石间，不复知有人世荣辱事。」《棠川郑氏宗谱》

楠溪江主流及其主要支流河床开阔，平坦和缓，形成36湾72滩。人们世代在滩地上植树造林，形成绵延数十公里的郁郁葱葱的滩林。

滩林与两岸村落、田园、山丘相交织掩映，形成清流、碧潭、河滩、草地、村落、远山、蓝天、白云层次极为丰富的山水林田园景观。

幼于其中从事生活劳作，时时处处诗情画意。

楠溪山水中的儒雅散淡、灵秀清纯，乡民的朴实诚恳和原乡文化的宜居家园，共同铸了和谐宁静的宜居家园。

Always full of poetic and picturesque charm

In the leisure time of reading and studying, playing the zither (a traditional Chinese musical instrument) and planting flowers bring the greatest joy. When the weather is clear, I fetch spring water to brew tea and enjoy it with a few close friends. Amidst the misty mountains and flowing waters, we seek happiness and freedom, no longer concerned about the successes and failures of life.

——Genealogy of the Zheng Family in Tangchuan

The riverbed of the main stream of Nanxi River and its main tributaries is wide, flat and gentle, forming 36 bays and 72 beaches. People have planted trees on the beach for generations, forming a lush beach forest that stretches for tens of kilometers.

The beach forest intersects with the villages, countryside, and hills on both sides of the river, forming a rich landscape of mountains, rivers, grasslands, villages, distant mountains, blue sky, and white clouds. Men, women, and children engage in daily life and work in it, always full of poetic and picturesque atmosphere. The pure and beautiful scenery of Nanxi, the simplicity and honesty of the villagers, and the elegance and simplicity of the original culture have all combined to create a harmonious and peaceful livable home.

耕隐翁非徒稼穑，由来种田兼种德。

明·李贽

中华秋沙鸭

白鹭

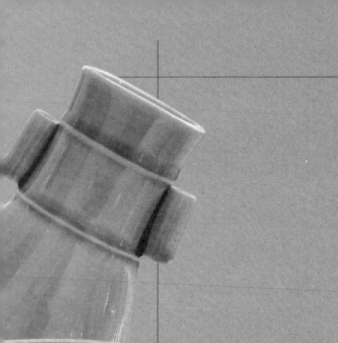

瓯越传承
Legacy of Ou-Yue

早在5000多年前的新石器时代，瓯越先民就已在楠溪江流域繁衍生息，这里至今仍保留着新石器时代的文化遗址。

两岸保存完好的大量宋代村落规划布局，明、清时期的民居建筑以及古塔、古桥、古亭、古牌楼等名胜古迹，更是研究价值高、观赏性强的人文景观。

Dating back more than 5,000 years to the Neolithic Age, the ancestors of the Ou-Yue (eastern Zhejiang Province) people thrived in the Nanxi River Basin. To this day, the region still preserves cultural relics from the Neolithic Period.

Along the banks, there are numerous well-preserved Song Dynasty (960-1279) village layouts, Ming (1368-1644) and Qing (1644-1911) Dynasty residential buildings, and historic relics such as ancient towers, bridges, pavilions, and archways. These cultural landmarks possess significant research value and offer captivating scenic views.

同时，难得的是，几经岁月洗礼，以及历史上数次拥有先进文化的中原居民的南迁，让这片土地拥有了极具古风的传统生活方式以及独特的文化灵魂，创造了独树一帜的永嘉文化，这种文化深厚隽永，守正创新，时至今日，那些千年沉淀下来的技艺与文脉，依然熠熠生辉。

Remarkably, after enduring the passage of time and multiple migrations of culturally advanced Central Plains residents, this land has preserved an ancient and distinctive way of life along with a unique cultural essence. This has given rise to the remarkable Yongjia culture, characterized by its deep roots, innovation, and enduring legacy. Even to this day, the craftsmanship and cultural heritage nurtured over thousands of years continue to radiate a brilliant light.

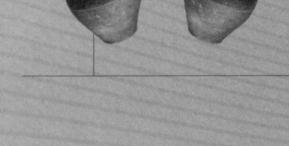

淬火瓯窑

OUYAO KILN
TEMPERED BY FIRE

引言

瓯窑是中国古代瓷窑，始于温州一带的瓯江两岸，发展于六朝，延及两宋，被誉为"温州东南的瓯窑瓷窑"。故浙江温州的瓯江两岸，西晋时期以其淡翠色的瓷器驰名遐迩，瓯窑青瓷以其独特的淡雅青色，权威指出是为中国青瓷之瑰宝。瓯窑以其最具代表性的"缥瓷"闻名于世，早期出现在东汉时期，活跃在两晋南北朝至唐代的条窑场，人们也把它称之为"瓯器"，习惯用在当时的茶道中，这是中国陶瓷所属，成为最早期出现及发展中的瓷场，是最具代表性的名窑之一。

2006年，永嘉县坦头村发现瓯窑遗址，揭开了瓯窑的神秘面纱。遗万件残器藏瑰宝，传统的瓯窑烧制工艺和瓷器，控制出为世人揭开了传承千年的瓯窑技艺和文化面纱。

有关资料表明，韩国、菲律宾与非洲等域的遗址中，海外均有所发现。

传承千年的瓯窑发展脉络，不仅可以观瞻窑至宋明时期人们的生活细节，也是永嘉历史上经济、文化繁荣昌盛的生动例证。

The Ouyao Kiln, an ancient Chinese porcelain kiln, originated in the Eastern Han Dynasty (25-220),developed during the Six Dynasties (220-589), and continued through the Song Dynasty. Located on both banks of the Oujiang River in present-day Wenzhou, Zhejiang Province, it was named after the river.

In the Western Jin Dynasty, poet Pan Yue (247-300) wrote in his"An Ode to the Musical Instrument Sheng"the lines . The word piao refers to the elegant light blue color of the Ouyao Kiln's porcelain.As a result, the blue-green porcelain produced by the kiln is known as "Piao Porcelain," the progenitor of Chinese blue-green porcelain. The Ouyao Kiln's Piao Porcelain had also become fashionable tableware for the nobles of the time. Another Jin Dynasty poet, Du Yu (?-311), mentioned in his "An Ode to Late-Picked Tea Leaves"that mention making the Ouyao Kiln in eastern Zhengjiang the earliest kiln site documented in the literature.In the Qing Dynasty, scholar Zhu Yan (around the end of the 18th century) mentioned in his "A Discussion on Porcelain" that the "later emerald peak" and "sky blue porcelain was developed on this"and that "the Ouyue Kiln was famous before the establishment of the Yuezhou Prefecture indicating its far-reaching influence.

In 2006, the remains of a Tang Dynasty Ouyao Kiln site were discovered in Tantou Village, Yongjia. Over ten thousand high-quality porcelain artifacts and a complete kiln structure were unearthed, revealing the mysterious legacy of the Ouyao Kiln to the world.

Available records show that Yongjia-produced Ouyao Kiln porcelain was exported overseas, with discoveries made in ancient shipwrecks in regions including Korea, the Philippines,and Africa.

The development of the Ouyao Kiln, spanning a thousand years,not only provides insights into the daily lives of people from the Wei and Jin Dynasties (220-420) to the Song and Ming Dynasties,but also stands as a vivid testament to the economic and cultural splendor that Yongjia has enjoyed throughout its history.

淬火瓯窑

Ouyao Kiln
Tempered By Fire

不拘一格，不落俗套

千百年来，永嘉人泼泉煮茶已成传统，空气中都弥漫着泉水丝丝的甜气。相传晋代山中宰相陶弘景曾在大若岩隐居修道多年，为汲取上佳山泉，陶公特地泛舟至此，取水煮茶。

楠溪江上等山水孕育了上等珍茶——乌牛早茶。乌牛早产于浙江省永嘉县乌牛街道一带，且是江南一带甚至最早上市的春茶，因此而得名。乌牛早茶外形扁平挺直，条索显，色泽绿翠光润，香气浓郁持久，滋味甘醇爽，汤色嫩绿明亮，叶底翠绿肥壮，匀齐成朵。乌牛早，芽叶肥壮，叶如雀舌。

好茶配好味，自古以来，这里也是温州的全羊，从源地，从朴实无华的发村头巷尾到大雅之堂，永嘉美食正如梅溪风物，从不拘一格，不落俗套，无论客自何方，都奉上

永嘉人向来以好客著称，无论自何方，都奉人心脾。茶食招待，带着山水的甘洌与市井的烟火，沁人

Be eclectic and unconventional

For thousands of years, people in Yongjia have been observing the tradition to brew tea with spring water, filling the air with the delicate sweetness of the springs. It is said that during the Jin Dynasty (265-420) prime minister Tao Hongjing once lived in seclusion at the Dar Kuo Yan for many years. In order to absorb the best mountain spring, Tao Gong went boating here and climbed the cliff by the edge of the stream to fetch water and brew tea.

The superior landscapes of the Nanxi River give birth to a premium tea known as Wuniu Early Tea. Wuniu Early Tea is produced in the Wuniu subdistrict of Yongjia County, Zhejiang Province, and is one of the earliest spring teas available in the region each year, hence its name.The tea features a flat, straight appearance with tight leaves covered in fine hairs. It is lustrously green with a lasting, rich fragrance and a sweet, refreshing taste. Its liquor is a bright, tender green, and the leaves are plump, even, and green.The tea leaves are shaped like bird's tongues, giving rise to the term "Wuniu Early Tea".

Yongjia people have always been renowned for their hospitality. Regardless of where the guests come from, they are treated with tea and food, offering the refreshing taste of the mountains and the lively atmosphere of the town, delighting the senses and invigorating the spirit.

 沁心茶食
REFRESHING TEA AND CUISINE

沁心茶食
REFRESHING TEA AND CUISINE

乌牛早茶

番薯枣

永嘉老酒汗

永嘉麦饼

锦粉饺

非遗承袭

INTANGIBLE CULTURAL HERITAGE

文化如酒，日久弥香

千古县永嘉，在漫长的历史岁月中，留下了许多宝贵的非物质文化遗产。

永嘉昆曲、永嘉乱弹等诸多曲艺形式在此传唱经久不衰，木雕、泥塑、竹编、剪纸、旗瓷、瓯绣等一系列千工艺项目又印证了永嘉人的勤劳与智慧。

文化如酒，日久弥香，沉淀下来的这些非遗项目，带着历史的痕迹，又不断吸收着新鲜血液，一代代非遗传承人，坚守这片净土，也在展望着光辉的明天。

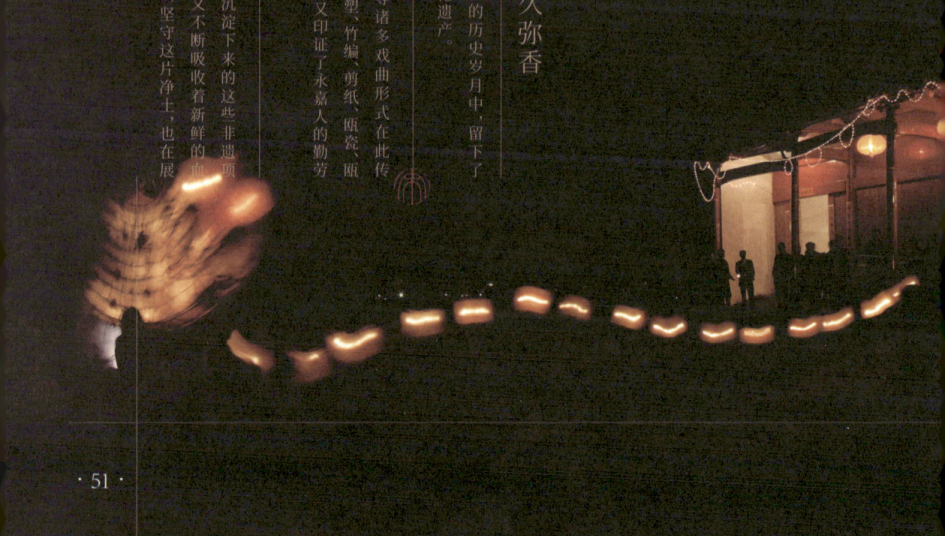

Inheritance of Intangible heritage cultural

Over the course of thousands of years, the ancient county of Yongjia has left behind many valuable intangible cultural heritages.

Yongjia kunqu Opera, Yongjia luantan, and other forms of traditional drama have been performed here for generations, remaining popular over time. The craftsmanship of wood carving, clay sculpture, bamboo weaving, paper cutting, Ou ceramics, and Ou embroidery further exemplifies the diligence and wisdom of Yongjia people.

Culture is like wine, becoming more fragrant over time. These intangible cultural heritage projects, steeped in history, continue to incorporate fresh ideas. Generation after generation of inheritors have guarded this pure land while looking forward to a bright future.

舞龙灯
dragon lantern dance

跑马灯
horse race lamp

布袋龙
Bagged Dragon

Bamboo carving 竹雕

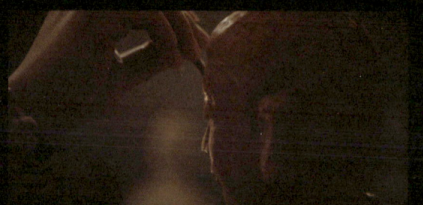

Clay sculpture 泥塑

Sugar shaping 糖塑

Puppet show 木偶戏

瓯绣 | Ouxiu

瓯绣 | Ouxiu

弹棉花 | Fluff cotton

非遗承袭

Ancient village And ancient rhyme

武术节 | Martial arts festival

木雕 | woodcarving

非遗承袭
Intangible cultural heritage

南戏昆韵
Southern Drama

南戏，又称"永嘉杂剧"，起源于北宋末年，具备完整的文学剧本和舞台演出体制，是中国戏曲最早的成熟形式。永嘉昆曲发源于南戏，因长期扎根于民间造就了表演质朴粗犷、行腔明快流畅的演出风格，被誉为研究南戏的"活化石"。到了清初，永嘉地区又产生了包括高腔、和调、正反乱弹等多种昆腔的剧种，称为"永嘉乱弹"。

质朴的永嘉人，骨子里就有着对戏曲文化的热爱，忙时插秧，闲时读文，日积月累，戏曲便沉淀为一种文化基因。时至今日，每逢佳节盛典、祭祀遗请时，戏台上的锣鼓喧天、余音绕梁与戏台下的观者如织、热闹欢腾经久未衰。

从田间地头的呼唱，到古戏台的闪亮，每一折永昆，每一曲乱弹，演绎的都是这片土地生长出来的生活。

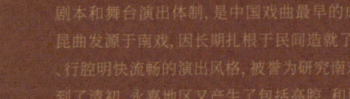

Nanxi Opera, also known as the Yongjia Zaju, originated in the late Northern Song Dynasty (960-1127). It boasts a complete literary script and stage performance system, making it the earliest mature form of Chinese opera. Yongjia kunqu opera, which originated from Nanxi Opera, features a rustic, rough, and smooth performance style due to its long history rooted in folk culture. It is considered a living "fossil" for studying Nanxi Opera. By the early Qing Dynasty, Yongjia had produced various forms of opera, including gaoqiang (a style of singing in Chinese operas characterized by high-pitched singing often accompanied by percussion instruments only), hediao (tuneful), zhengfan luantan, and others, collectively known as Yongjia luantan.

The people of Yongjia, known for their simplicity and sincerity, have an innate passion for opera culture. Whether occupied with rice planting during busy times or indulging in opera during leisure moments, the art form has gradually become an integral part of their cultural heritage. Even to this day, during festive occasions, ceremonies, and ritual performances, the resounding beats of gongs and drums fill the air on the stage, while the audience below, in a joyous and lively ambiance, remains as enthusiastic and captivated as ever.

From the humming in the fields to the brilliance of the ancient opera stage, each act of Yongjia kunqu and every tune of luantan tells the story of life on this land.

永昆·荆钗记

永昆·杀狗记

永昆·琵琶记

永昆·张协状元

古村社戏
Local operas in ancient village

永嘉乱弹
Yongjia Luantan

木偶戏
Marionette

古村古韵

Ancient Villages With A

生活在楠溪江流域村落的家族各自的"家训"、"家谱"都有关于"耕读"的记载。"耕读传家"是永嘉人自古以来受到的教诲，中国的"耕读文化"是半耕半读的世外桃源式理想生活的文化表现。在楠溪江古村落的家谱里记载着"耕以致富，读可荣身"，"耕"是经济基础，"读"是考取功名，可光宗耀祖。

在一江秀水的滋润下，楠溪江两岸人才辈出。从唐朝至清朝，永嘉一共出过711位进士；两宋时期，这里出现"永嘉学派"、"永嘉四灵"，在中国文化史上占有一席之地。

Every family living in the villages along the Nanxi River has their own "family precepts" and "family genealogies" that include records about "cultivating and learning." "Cultivating and learning for generations" is the guidance that Yongjia people have received since ancient times. China's "cultivating and learning culture" represents an idyllic, utopian lifestyle of balancing agriculture with education. The genealogical records of the ancient Nanxi River villages contain passages such as "cultivate to prosper, learn to honor one's person." "Cultivate" refers to the economic foundation, while "learn" signifies the pursuit of scholarly achievements that bring pride to one's ancestors.

Nurtured by the enchanting waters of the river, the banks of the Nanxi River have given rise to a multitude of talented individuals. From the Tang Dynasty to the Qing Dynasty, Yongjia had produced a total of 711 successful candidates for the imperial examinations at the highest level. During the Song Dynasty, the "Yongjia School" and the "Four Poets of Yongjia" emerged, holding an important place in Chinese cultural history.

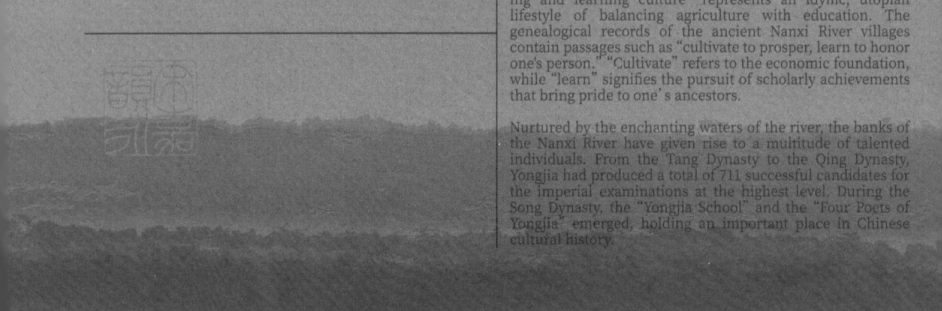

我最爱楠溪江的乡土建筑。
爱就爱它们的既极其朴素粗蛮，又极其精致细腻。
——陈志华

I love the vernacular buildings of the Nanxi River the most.
I love them for their simplicity and crudeness, yet also for their exquisite intricacy.
– Chen Zhihua

More than 200 ancient single-surname bloodline villages are scattered along the banks of the Nanxi River.

To this day, they still contain a large number of Neolithic cultural sites, as well as ancient towers, bridges, roadside pavilions, archways, and battlefields from the Tang, Song, Yuan (1206-1368), Ming, and Qing dynasties. These villages also retain a leisurely way of life where men farm and women weave, living in leisure and almost self-sufficient.

In addition, the ancestral villages of the Zong clan have preserved a spiritual legacy that instills in the people of Yongjia a deep respect for teachers and a philosophy of living in harmony with the world. It is precisely this cultivation of character and unique natural landscape that has given birth to one long-lived village after another in the Nanxi River region, earning Yongjia the reputation as a "land of longevity" worldwide.

古村古韵
Ancient Villages
with Ancient Rhymes

古村古韵
·Ancient Villages with Ancient Rhymes·

古村古韵
"Ancient Villages with Ancient Rhymes"

古村古韵

Ancient Villages with Ancient Rhymes

中国长寿之村

Home of longevity in China

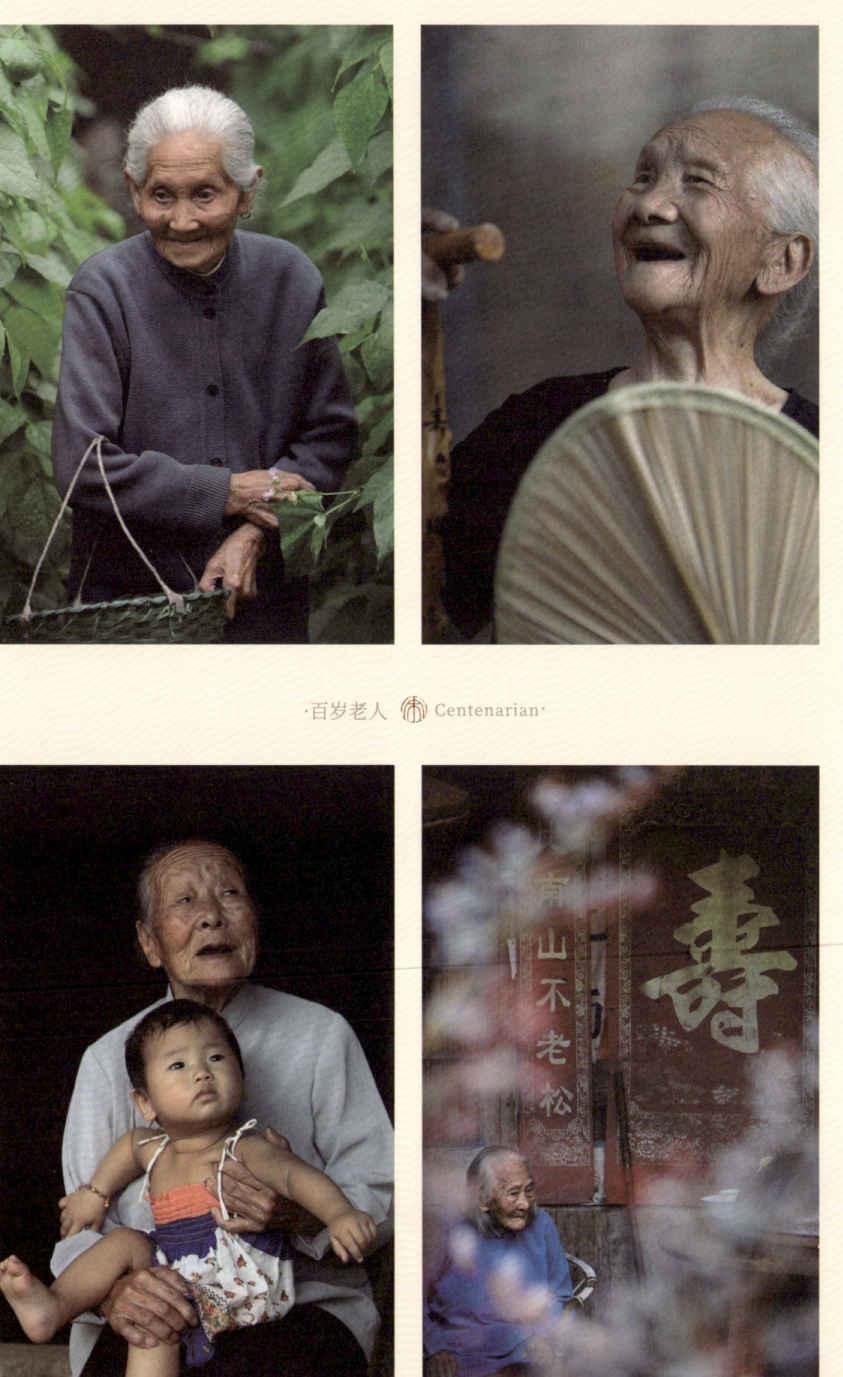

·百岁老人 · Centenarian·

JIANGNAN SONG VILLAGE

江南宋村

楠溪江畔，江南宋村

楠溪江中、上游的村庄，多盛于两宋期间的精英家族移民。表山、芙蓉、苍坡、岭北、枫林、花坦等建于北宋，溪头、岩头、蓬溪等建于南宋，廿等建于北宋。

楠溪江古村落的建筑风格，保留了宋派建筑的风格，这在中国民居建筑中算是一个孤本。如果说杭州是宋城的范本，那么楠溪江古村落，便是宋村的宋城本，可称之为江南第一宋村。这些建筑大多以木、盘石为村，少作修饰，各有一种天然之美，原正源于宋朝天人极高的审美眼光。天人合一的理念，各具匠心地融造出村落又依自身地特点，独具匠心地酿造出各自的设计理念，如形似七星八斗的芙蓉村、文房四宝苍坡村、"金山前水头"等村。

今日，这里已不仅仅是过往历史岁月的见证，更吸引着越来越多的当代年轻人到访此地，在楠溪江畔，江南宋村寻求内心的平静与美学的真谛。

Nanxi River bank, Jiangnan Song Village

The villages in the middle and upper reaches of the Nanxi River were mostly settled by elite families who migrated during the Northern and Southern Song Dynasties. Baishan, Furong, Cangpo, Yubei, Fenglin, and Huatan are among the villages that originated during the Northern Song Dynasty, while Xikou, Yantou, and Pengxi were established during the Southern Song Dynasty.

The architectural style of the Nanxi River's ancient villages preserves the style of Song Dynasty architecture, which is unique among Chinese dwellings. If Hangzhou can be considered a model of a Song Dynasty city, then the ancient villages of the Nanxi River can be considered models of Southern Song Dynasty villages, earning the title of "the top song dynasty villages in the lower reaches of the Yangtze River." Most of these buildings use raw wood and rough stone as materials, with minimal decoration, exuding a natural beauty that stems from the Song Dynasty's highly refined aesthetic sensibilities. The layout of the villages often adheres to the concept of "unity of heaven and humanity," with each village crafting its own unique design concept based on its specific topography. Examples include Furong Village's "seven stars and eight dippers," Cangpo Village's "four treasures of the study," and Yantou Village's "golden mountain and beautiful water."

Today, it is not just a testament to the history of the past. They also draw an increasing number of contemporary young people to visit, seeking inner tranquility and the true essence of aesthetics along the Nanxi River, amidst the picturesque Song Dynasty villages of Jiangnan, situated at the lower reaches of the Yangtze River.

江南宋村
Jiangnan Song Village

江南宋村

Jiangnan Song Village

水如棋局分街陌，山似屏帏绕画楼。

北宋·杨蟠

渔火遍连市，村庐半掩柴。 ——北宋·赵抃

江南宋村

Jiangnan Song Village

江 南 宋 村
Jiangnan Song Village

JIANGNAN SONG VILLAGE

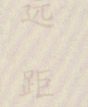

江南宋村

楠溪江畔，江南宋村

今日，这里已不仅仅代表着来自过去的纪念，更吸引着越来越多的当代年轻人到访此地。在楠溪江畔，江南宋村，寻求内心的平静与美学的真谛。

Nanxi River bank
Jiangnan Song Village

Today, these places serve as more than mere witnesses to the accumulated history of bygone years. They also draw an increasing number of contemporary young people to visit, seeking inner tranquility and the true essence of aesthetics along the Nanxi River, amidst the picturesque Song Dynasty villages of Jiangnan, situated at the lower reaches of the Yangtze River.

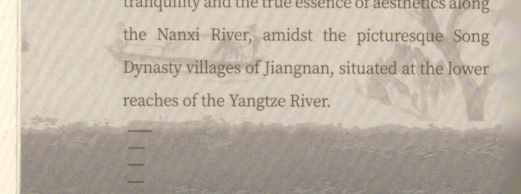

A MODERN PANORAMIC VIEW OF THE SONG DYNASTY VILLAGES

A MODERN PANORAMIC VIEW OF THE SONG DYNASTY VILLAGES

A MODERN PANORAMIC VIEW OF THE SONG DYNASTY VILLAGE

编委会

顾　　问：黄慧 吴呈钱 胡宝峰 王晓雄

主　　任：张贤孟 周旭丹

副 主 任：胡程远 单爱东 吴学龙 徐俊 刘晓丽 郑良 徐文凯

委　　员：施太永 郑贺龙 吕洲

编辑部

主　　编：周旭丹

责任主编：单爱东

策　　划：施太永 周超扬

撰　　稿：周超扬 董璐瑶

编　　辑：颜冬冬 滕宏鸥

特约编辑：叶卫周 张则斌 陈凯 杨伟兴

校　　对：郑贺龙 吕洲

篆　　刻：陈元子

设计制作：杭州西陌文化传媒有限公司

摄　　影（按姓氏笔画排列）：丁剑鸣 大佑 王少敏 叶卫周

叶新仁 孙岳胜 刘晓峰 吴加勤 邹黎霞 杨伟兴 杨爽 陈光武

张则斌 何建勇 周乐见 周良东 周园 周丽芳 金亦武 金江彬

金肖武 金建国 金强 林志彬 胡永东 胡国 胡冠荣 胡臻 郝

远征 徐永义 徐苍峰 徐时涛 徐慧芬 谢文东 虞若飞 滕宏鸥

戴亚琼

鸣　　谢：温州市楠溪江旅游经济发展中心

永嘉县摄影家协会

中共永嘉县委宣传部出品

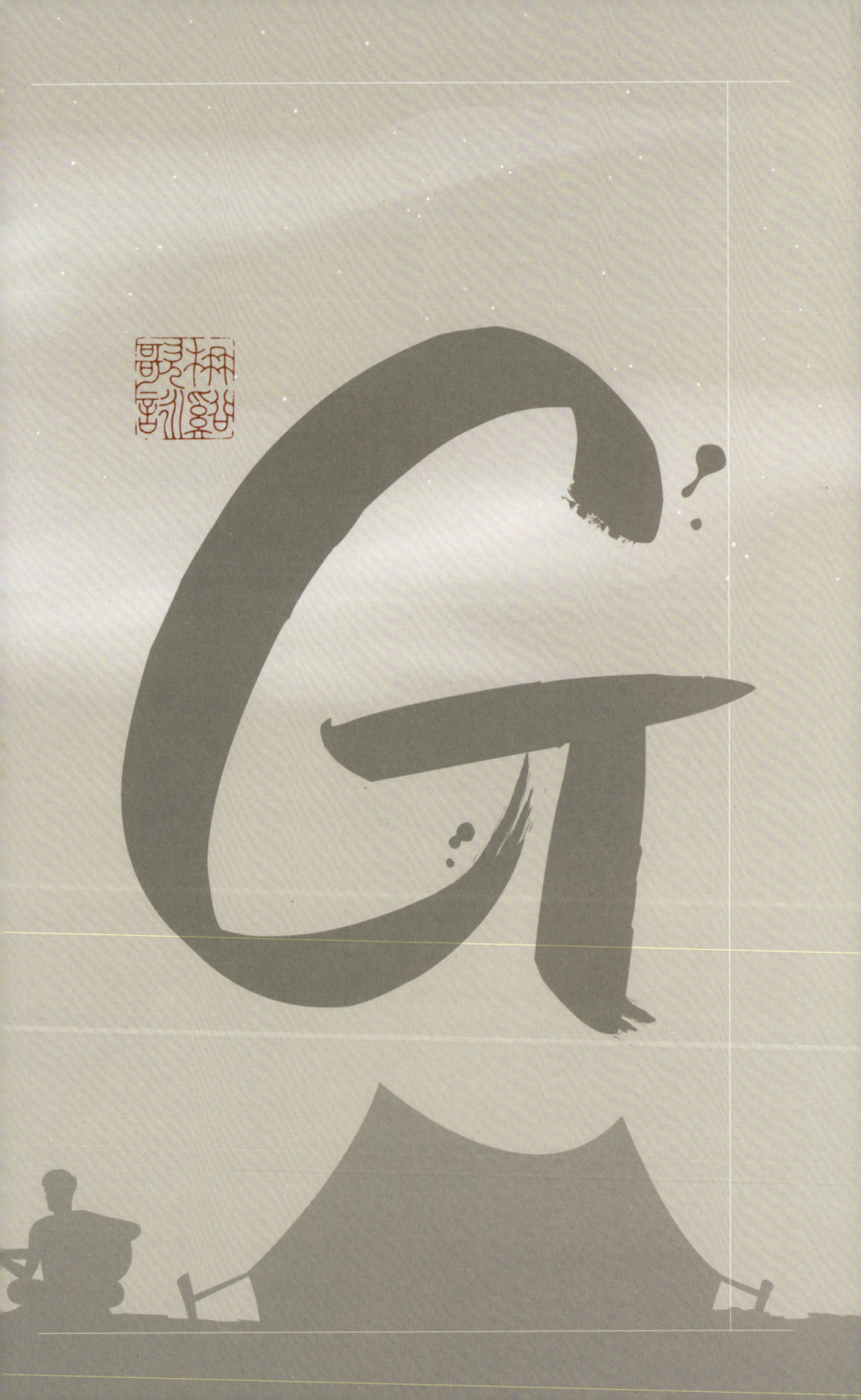

GALAXY

楠溪的夜, 漫天星海, 如梦如幻;

楠溪的夜, 对酒当歌, 人生几何。

青石板上, 千年斑驳绘成华彩图卷,

宋村回眸, 遇见未来的自己。

Nanxi's night, adorned with a galaxy of stars, is dreamlike and surreal;
Nanxi's night, where people raise their glasses and sing,
On the ancient bluestone slabs, a vivid tapestry unfolds.
Song Cun Looking Back and Meeting your Future Self.

NOSTALGI

楠溪江民宿

楠溪江民宿

An overview of homestays in the Nanxi River region

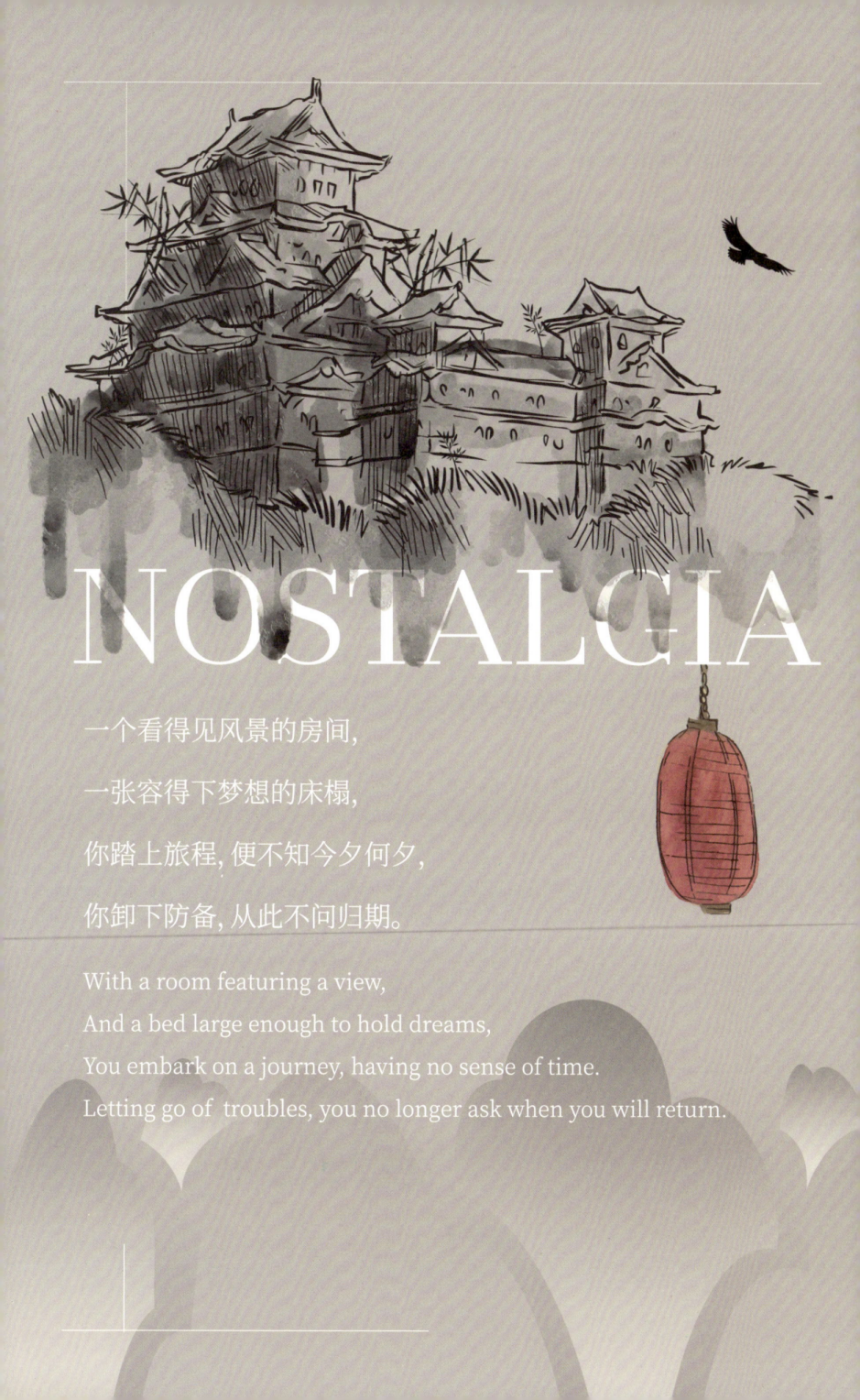

MUSIC/ SLOW CITY/ FOLK SONG/ NATIVE LAND/

音乐漫都 民谣故土

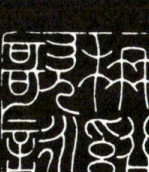

MUSIC/ SLOW CITY/ FOLK SONG/ NATIVE LAND/

音乐漫都 民谣故土

音乐漫都、民谣故土；
南曲北唱、摇滚复兴。
这片宽厚的山水，兼容并蓄，包罗万象，
这片沉静的土地，正迸发出这个时代的最强音。

It is a haven for music and a birthplace of folk songs;
Where melodies from the south and north intertwine,
igniting a resurgence of rock and roll.
This expansive and inclusive land encompasses everything.
This serene soil now unleashes the mightiest sound of this era.

MUSIC/ SLOW CITY/ FOLK SONG/ NATIVE LAND/

音乐漫都 民谣故土

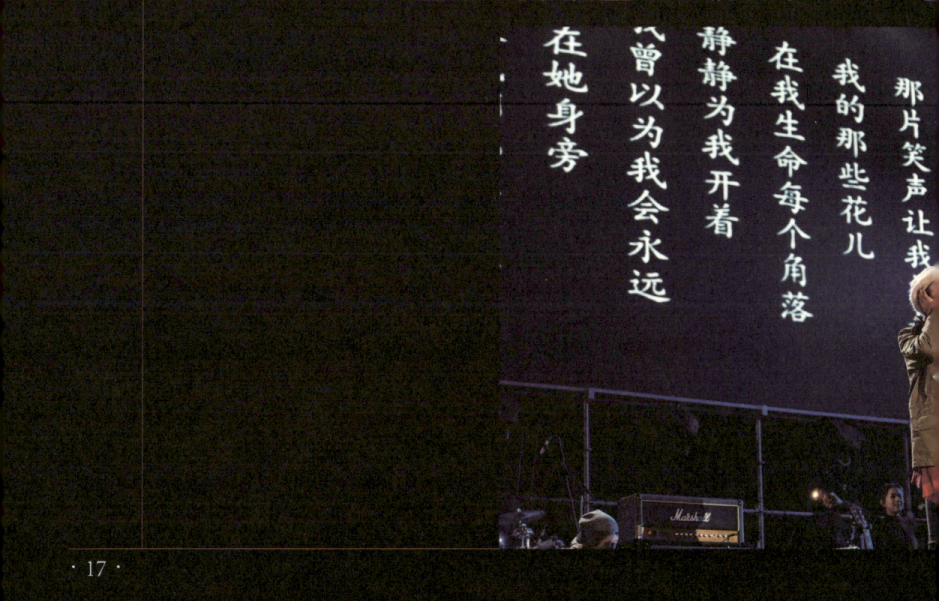

OPEN

音乐漫都、民谣故土；

南曲北唱、摇滚复兴。

这片宽厚的山水，兼容并蓄，包罗万象，

这片沉静的土地，正迸发出这个时代的最强音。

It is a haven for music and a birthplace of folk songs;

Where melodies from the south and north intertwine, igniting a resurgence of rock and roll.

This expansive and inclusive land encompasses everything.

This serene soil now unleashes the mightiest sound of this era.

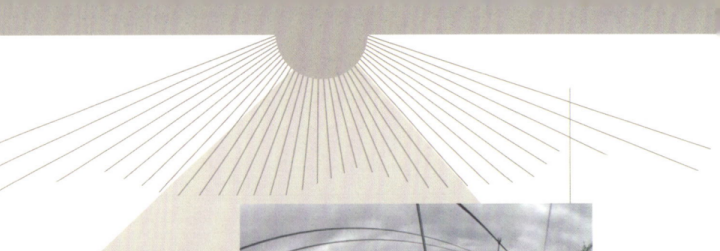

SUNSHINE

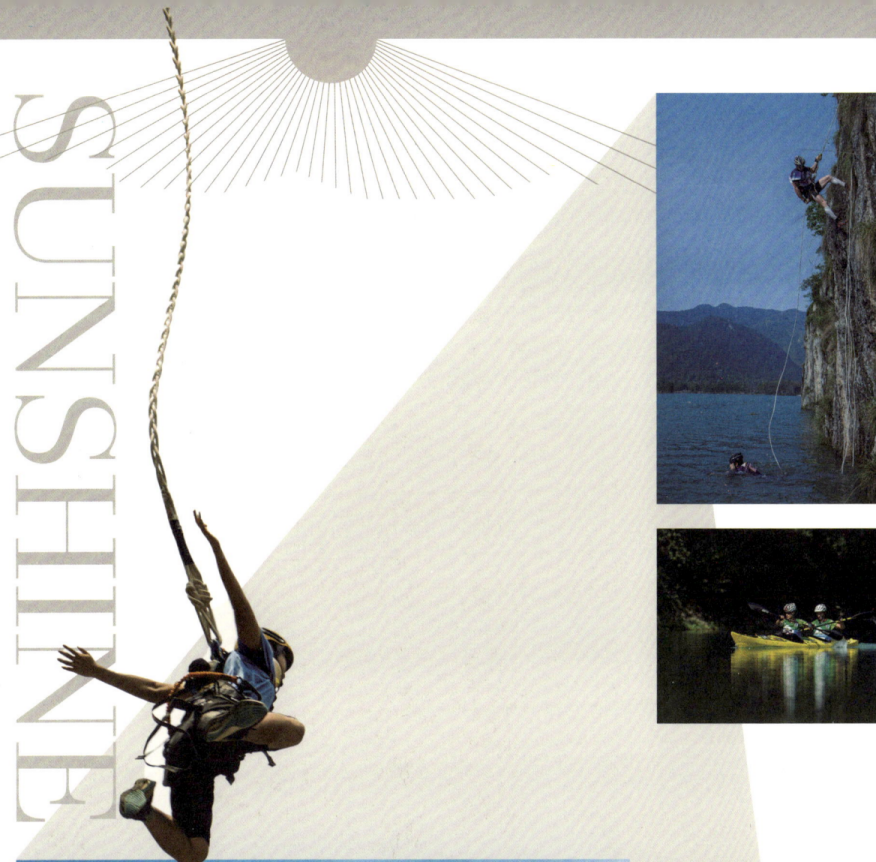

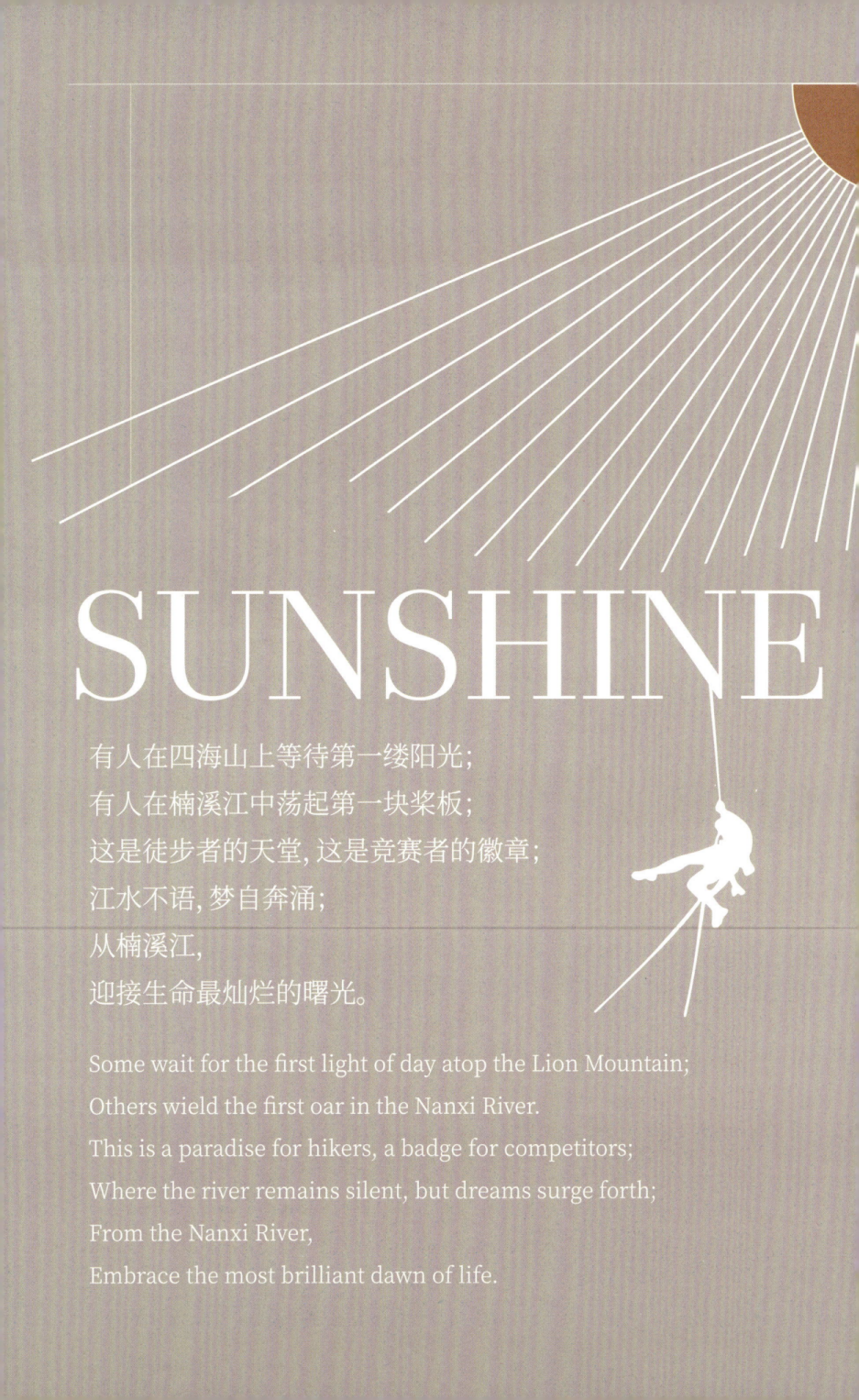

朝茶夕舞, 跃动山野
SONG, 是青春的歌咏

ugh Millennia

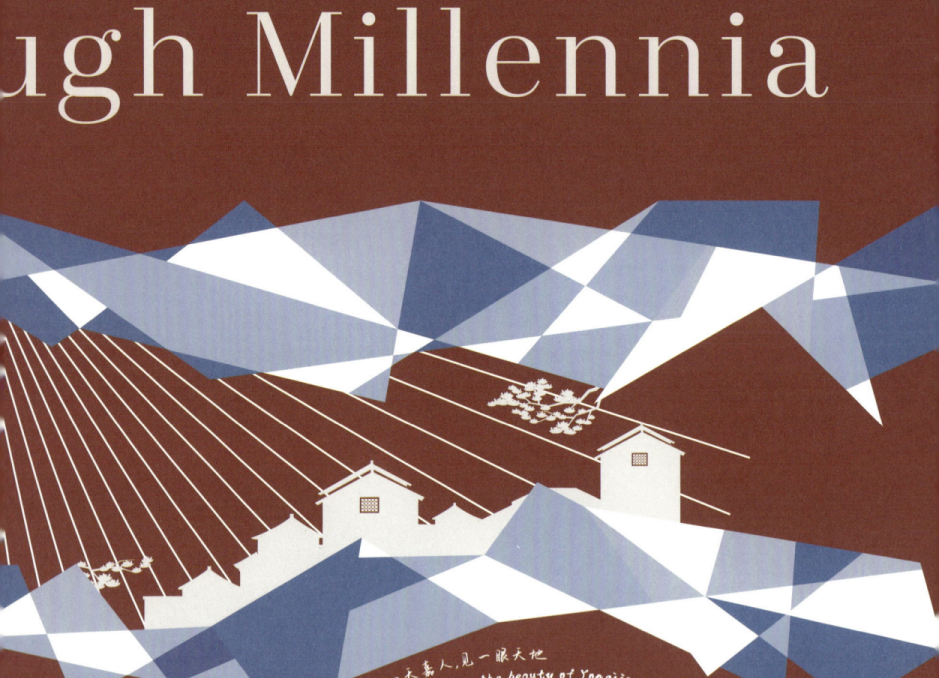

Enjoy the beauty of Yongjia and feel a different experience

YONGJIA NANXI RIVER

Yongjia County, under the jurisdiction of Wenzhou City, Zhejiang Province, China, has a history of more than 1800 years, which is the historical root and cultural source of Wenzhou. The total area is 2677.64 square kilometers, with 7 subdistrict, 11 towns, and 4 townships under its jurisdiction. It has golden business cards such as "Hometown of Longevity in China", "Hometown of Pumps and Valves in China", "Capital of Buttons in China", "Hometown of Zippers in China", and "Capital of Toys in China". It is the fourth largest county in Zhejiang Province, the largest county in Wenzhou, the first batch of coastal open counties in China, a major county for Chinese cultural tourism, a millennium old county in China, and an old revolutionary base county in Zhejiang.

Today's Yongjia is the forefront of the integration of the Yangtze River Delta and the "bridgehead" of Wenzhou's integration with Hangzhou and Shanghai. It is brave and energetic; It is a highland for industrial clusters and technological innovation, integrating with the river and integrating industry and city; It is the preferred tourist destination for beautiful China and a holy land for rural music in China, full of vitality and endless flow.

Which means to be forever in the ancient Chinese language.

一瞬千年

A Glimpse thro

 希望之城——永嘉

永嘉县,隶属中国浙江省温州市,有着1800多年建县史,是温州的历史之根、文化之源,总面积2677.64平方公里，下辖7街道11镇4乡,拥有"中国长寿之乡","中国泵阀之乡","中国纽扣之都","中国拉链之乡","中国玩具之都"等金名片。是浙江省县城面积第四大县、温州第一大县,也是全国首批沿海对外开放县、中国文化旅游大县、中国千年古县、浙江老革命根据地县。

 今天的永嘉,是长三角一体化的前沿阵地、温州融杭接沪的"桥头堡",勇为人先,活力无限;是产业集群、科技创新的高地,拥江融入,产城融合;是美丽中国首选旅游目的地,中国乡村音乐圣地,涌动生机,奔流不息。

这就是永嘉,用心用情,永受嘉福。

S	Sunshine 阳光	03.
O	Open 开放	13.
N	Nostalgia 乡愁	27.
G	Galaxy 银河系	41.